THE JUDO ROLL
THE GENTLE ART OF NEGOTIATION

For Attorneys by an Attorney

By Chris Lisle

FOREWORD

Most lawyers would agree that many cases should and could be settled on the front end, but it's rarely done. Despite the fact that 95% of all cases settle, most cases settle "on the court house steps" after years of needless and expensive litigation not beneficial to either client. Why? Each lawyer blames the other for not picking up the phone.

In the end, too many attorneys depend on mediators to do the "heavy lifting" of negotiating their case for them, but as the old saying goes, if you want something done right do it yourself. Great attorneys do reach out because they always have their client's best interest in mind and always retain personal command of their client's case. They have no fear to pick up a phone and call the other side and speak openly and candidly. Negotiating is not a sign of weakness.

This pamphlet is intended to impart the basic skills to be a great negotiator. It is based on the experiences of twenty-six years of practice, the last two of which were spent as the lead

negotiator for Walmart handling direct resolution of personal

injury claims. In that time, I was able to personally negotiate and

successfully resolve hundreds of personal injury claims including

wrongful deaths and traumatic brain injuries.

Negotiation is a skill which can be learned and beneficial

to you personally, professionally, and your clients.

TABLE OF CONTENTS

The Art of Negotiation – the Judo ROLL

Why learn negotiation? Negotiation is a life skill, not just a skill for resolving lawsuits. We do it every day with loved ones, friends, at work, with the people we meet. It is a skill that can be learned. If you learn to master the art of negotiation, you learn to master the daily conflicts in your life.

Negotiation is the art of reaching agreement, and a "negotiator" is "someone whose job it is to try to help two groups who disagree with each other to reach an agreement" *Cambridge Dictionaries.* In practice, negotiation is the **art of persuasion**. Persuasion is "The act of influencing the mind by arguments or reasons offered, or by anything that moves the mind or passions, or inclines the will to a determination." *Marx vs. Threet*, 131 Ala. 340, 30 So. 831, *Black's Law Dictionary*, 2nd Ed.

Negotiation is a skill that can be learned and mastered as an art. If one remembers the **Judo ROLL**, they will begin to master both the skill and art of negotiation. The Judo "Roll" is an acronym for: (1) Relationship, (2) Objective Fairness, (3) Listening, and (4) Levers of Negotiation.

Relationship

Establishing a working "relationship" is the heart of the art in reaching a settlement. A positive working relationship allows two parties to negotiate differences of substance. The relationship begins with the first contact and continues to the last contact. It is a constant process. To establish and maintain an "effective" negotiating relationship, every contact must be "soft on the person, firm on the problem." Every contact should convey honesty, fairness, and respect. Never say, write or do anything you will regret. Assume everything you say, do or write is recorded and will be played back to the judge, jury or on the evening news.

There is truth to the idea of negotiation Karma that you get what you give. If you are fair, they will be fair. If you are reasonable, they will be reasonable. If you listen, they listen. Yelling and anger are disrespectful, and beget yelling and disrespect.

Studies show that approximately 60% of all communication is non-verbal, 30% is tone, and 10% the words we use. Many negotiations are over the phone, so tone of voice is 90% of communication. Regardless of whether the negotiation is in person or over the phone, the tone of voice is critical and from it people infer hidden meaning. Insure that your tone of voice is working for you, not against you.

Small Talk Gets Big Results

Small talk is important to forming a relationship. There is a saying that "small talk gets big results." All studies show that small talk helps establish a working "relationship" by beginning a rapport with your opponent. Do not force small talk, but take the opportunity instead to engage in it when it is presented – it always is. For example, if your opponent says, "I'm sorry I didn't get back with you sooner I was out on vacation," take the opportunity to ask, "Where did you go?" You will learn to see the other person as a human and when you humanize each other you begin the process of trusting one another.

Practice Pointer: The negotiator's reputation

Reputation is either a shadow covering you in suspicion or a warm light inviting discussion. To be successful, a negotiator needs a reputation for honesty and fairness in every negotiation. There are times when an opposing party is none of these things, but even in those situations, if a negotiator maintains his/her reputation via effective communication, honesty and fairness, while showing respect, a good negotiator can reach a good settlement despite a non-reciprocal opposing counsel.

Objective Fairness

Fairness requires special emphasis. "Fairness" is the key to keeping all sides talking and not leaving the table. If emotions get out of hand, is hard to keep people talking. We know this to be true in our every day experiences, no one listen when they are mad. People are born with the "fight or flight" syndrome and this syndrome affects negotiations. If your opponent perceives your offers as "unfair" aka arbitrary, it will literally incite a physical response to "fight" you meaning argue with you. This is why all your actions must project fairness. If not, the negotiation is likely to fail. Fairness includes respect for the other party, the art of listening and the use of objective criteria to value claims and not appearing arbitrary in the offers you make.

Avoid your opponent's "fight" response by being objectively fair. How? If your opponent knows the basis for your offer, there's a better chance it will be considered "fair," even if they don't agree with it. If considered fair, they will continue to negotiate with you and shout, bang the table, and run out of the room. For example, don't simply offer $5,000.00 for an injury.

Always take the time to explain "I've considered the $1,500 in medical bills. I understand she has $500 in lost wages, and I'm adding to that for her claim of pain and suffering putting a value on this claim of $5,000.00). An offer without explanation is deemed arbitrary and unfair.

You will see later how objective fairness and "levers of negotiation" are the same. Fairness means that when you begin negotiating using your negotiation levers, you always speak in the common language of liability or damages when presenting offers.

Listen
Never Miss an Opportunity to be Quiet

Always listen! Never miss a good opportunity to be quiet! As the Dalai Lama said "When you talk, you are only repeating what you already know. But if you listen, you may learn something new." Do not go into a settlement discussion talking, begin by listening to the other side. Do not begin a negotiation with the false assumption you understand either

liability or damages. If you do, you will not listen. The other side

always has information you don't have. Find out what that

information is for it may change your opinion. Ask lots of open

ended questions. If they know you sincerely listen, they will talk

to you. What they tell you may either change your risk analysis

or concede facts that hurt their case and can be used as

negotiation levers by you.

The negotiator understands a demand is an offer to

compromise not an offer to fight. Never forget that actions

speak louder than words. If they wanted to fight, they wouldn't

be negotiating with you or sending you a nasty demand letter.

Too often people get upset by threatening oral demands or

letters. Good negotiators don't. Strongly worded statements or

letters are intended to influence the emotions of the person

receiving it, to increase their risk analysis by "scaring" them, but

in the end, it is an offer to compromise. A demand is a

temporary positional statement of a party; it is a means to a perceived settlement value based on known facts and current temporal interests of the parties at the time it is made. Strong emotional wording or threats in a demand are a simple negotiation tactic used since the dawn of mankind by kids and adults. Remember, negotiation is all about human decision making. The negotiator's job is to move through that positional statement and uncover the opposing party's real settlement position.

Why do a say a demand letter is a temporary position? Because demands go up or down over time. They are always temporary because the needs of the four parties constantly change (more on this later). Risks differ with each individual and differ for each individual at any point in time. The risk to the plaintiff and the risk to their attorney are different. One may need money now for bills unrelated to the claim, whereas the other may not. So, needs are based on time, and time is a "risk" factor for all parties. Each individual in a negotiation has different needs, different risk tolerances.

A demand tells the negotiator a lot about the person and claim, by either what is said or not said. If a demand has a deadline, timing is important. How can this be used by the negotiator to resolve the claim? If the demand gives a "take it or leave it" number, find out why and how that this figure was derived? The "take it or leave it number" gives important clues as to the interests of both the attorney and their client making the demand.

Practice Pointer: Key Points of Listening

1. Effective listening satisfies the other side's emotional interest to be heard and then, they will be able to listen to you;

2. You can listen without agreeing;

3. Gain useful information when listening and knowledge is negotiating power.

Practice Pointer: Effective Listening Behaviors

1. Paraphrase what they said without agreeing. This insures you have understood;

2. Inquire with open ended questions. Illicit what you don't know. They may be making assumptions which means there is risk if they are wrong or they may have facts that you don't have. Either is important;

3. Acknowledge their feelings, their tone, to demonstrate your understanding.

Levers for Negotiation

After one has established a relationship, listened and understands the other side and the facts of their case, then they can begin the negotiation. Always speak with respect and in the language of negotiation, meaning the common language of litigation to remain objectively fair. In litigation, and this means you speak in the common language of liability which is the jury instruction on liability. What does the law require? Is it a pure comparative state? Contributory negligence state? The common language of damages is speaking in terms of what that state allows and what the evidence shows. What is the standard for punitive? What do the facts show?

Practice Pointer- Don't Say Can't

Can't is a negative. It implies you don't have authority. Crisis negotiators never tell a hostage taker "we can't." No matter how crazy the demand, they don't say, "can't." For example, if someone holding hostages says, "I want a plane and $10 million dollars in an hour," the hostage negotiator won't say, "I can't." They will say, "I need more time," or "I need you to do this for me."

You must convey you are the right person to talk to and that, with the right evidence, the negotiator can resolve the case. If the negotiator says, "I can't," that implies they aren't the right person. "I've got all the authority you need if you get me the right evidence."

The Four Interests in Every Negotiation

To understand the art of settling a case, one must understand the financial motivations of all parties in wanting to settle. The four parties are the plaintiff, the plaintiff's attorney, the defendant, and defense counsel. Settlements always involve money and all parties eventually settle for the same reason – financial interest. The Plaintiff wants to recover money; plaintiff's counsel wants to make money and recover the costs and expenses advanced or not incur them; defense counsel makes money by defending and maintaining a future relationship with the client, and the defendant wants to save money, by paying as little as possible, with recognition it will have to pay something even if it's the cost of defense.

What is Settlement Value?

Remember, value is always temporary, so for all sides, the settlement value is the dollar value of the case that exceeds the risk of going to trial at any point in time during the evolution of a case. It is almost always fluid, as it is based on current costs, known risks and interests of the parties. It is temporal. It creates opportunities for compromise on all sides.

Determining Settlement Value, Yours and Theirs

Initial settlement value takes into consideration both the "costs" and "risk" of trial. "Costs" includes financial cost of the litigation (attorney fees, expenses, and expert costs), cost to company/party reputation, cost of a parties time away from work, the emotional cost to the party (family cases, death cases), the risk of prolonged litigation on the party (interest accruing on medical bills, risk of collection, risk of loss of evidence, etc). Beyond the "costs" of going to trial, the "risk" of trial is the risk of attaining a particular jury verdict in a particular venue. How good is the liability and what are average verdicts in this county for this type of case? There are many jury verdict research tools that assist with this calculation. In more serious cases, one would consider personal experience on these types of cases in this venue and in front of this judge. Judges have known judicial bents and how they rule and what they will allow a jury to hear or not hear affects the value of a case that must be considered.

The party's initial settlement value is derived before negotiating, but this isn't a final value for settlement purposes. But remember, don't go into a negotiation thinking you have it all figured out. A final settlement value isn't reached until after discussing the case with opposing counsel to insure all the facts and risks are understood, and nothing is ever fully understood. Opposing counsel may disclose a fact which changes the evaluation for better or for worse.

When do Negotiations begin?

Negotiation begins with the first contact with opposing counsel, whether that contact is the first pleading, email, phone call, etc. Every communication is a step towards eventual resolution.

Generally, negotiations are initiated with a "demand" from a plaintiff but can be initiated with an "offer" from the defendant. In either case, one should insure the demand or offer is protected by Rule of Evidence 408 by including the language of Rule 408 in their demand or offer.

Below is a sample settlement offer from a hypothetical defense counsel regarding a hypothetical slip and fall which touches on all aspects of the Judo ROLL. It begins with a process for confidential settlement discussions to take place, provide a framework for those discussions (time/manner/parties involved), establish a relationship with opposing counsel by introducing the negotiator, the negotiator's intent, a time table for resolving the case which introduces risk and parameters, and a brief discussion of substance without argument (showing an openness to discuss), and makes an initial offer to show fairness if enough information is available to do so. Keep in mind that all offers must written with the belief that plaintiff's counsel will share them with their clients as they are supposed to do. The offer should be written in a way that conveys your sincerity, as if you were sitting in a mediation speaking to the plaintiff.

<u>This communication is made in an effort to compromise a disputed claim and is intended to be confidential and protected under FRCP 408 and state law counterparts.</u>

(This establishes a "process" in that it establishes this communication as a protected settlement discussion. It conveys your intent to settle but recognition it may not, the injection of risk)

Hi _____,

My name is _____. I am an attorney representing _____. This is an attempt to settle the above ongoing case. As such, all communications from me should be considered confidential offers of compromise/settlement discussions and privileged under the applicable Rules of Civil Procedure. If we are not able to settle, then we will not be bound by this offer of compromise.

This paragraph introduces the negotiator (establish relationship). It also provides a process for resolution with direct communication and a time frame. It conveys intent but maintains risk of trial if they don't want to work with us.

I begin by saying we are sorry to hear about this accident. I hope you will convey to your client, along with our offer, our desire for a speedy and complete recovery.

This paragraph is the beginning of rapport/relationship. It is non-adversarial and intended to convey our intent to settle, not to fight, and hopefully, if shared with the plaintiff, will reduce any emotion that we don't care.

I understand _____ is ____ years old. I understand she slipped and fell on a clear liquid by the register. We don't know what it was or how long it was there. I understand she left the store, and later went to the ER where she was diagnosed with sprains/strains. Her pain continued, and an MRI showed a disc bulge at the L4/L5 noting a degenerative change but no acute findings. Her gross medical bills are $__k and the claims office offered $__k. You demanded $__k.

This statement of facts is general, non argumentative, no statement as to who is right or wrong, and so general as to not be argumentative and simply demonstrate show you have some understanding of the file and are willing to discuss (bc you are not argumentative). Importantly, it doesn't disclose any information you have that they don't!

I hope to visit with you by phone to discuss this more in depth, but based on what I understand, I offer $_____ to settle all disputed claims in full (inclusive of all liens). This is an offer to settle all claims, known or unknown, against all parties, known or unknown.

This offer is conditioned on you and your client agreeing to keep the terms of the settlement confidential to the extent allowed by law and on you and your firm paying any liens out of the settlement proceeds. Any ERISA, Medicare, Medicaid or other similar liens must be resolved in compliance with necessary regulatory provisions and may require withholding and paying those liens separately out of the settlement proceeds. In the event Plaintiff is eligible for Medicare, or will be within 18 months, your firm must provide a formal CMS final demand for payment letter (not just a conditional payment letter), prior to disbursement of the entire settlement proceeds. This letter must be provided even if the amount ultimately owed to Medicare is zero.

This paragraph specifically says "I hope to visit with you by phone" to demonstrate you are open to negotiation and inviting that negotiation. It shows you are willing to listen and get the whole picture. If they believe you are open, they will call back. The initial offer has to be "fair." If not, you will not be considered fair and the negotiation is likely to fail.

Please understand that if we are unable to resolve this case, we will not remain bound by this offer or any others. We are, however, committed to trying to resolve this fairly if possible.

This paragraph again keeps risk to the plaintiff in the picture and makes it clear this is a process unrelated to litigation. If the case doesn't settle, they will have to litigate and incur significant time and expense.

The First Phone Call
Establishing a Relationship

The first phone call will not settle the claim, but will establish a relationship to do so. First impressions are lasting impressions, and the "tone" of this first phone call sets the tone for all future discussions. Tone of voice is the way they will "see" you and judge you. If this phone call doesn't go well, you may kill the ability to settle the claim at a later date. A positive phone call will hopefully open the door of opportunity to resolve the case by getting your opponent out of the "fight" mode of litigation and into the "settlement" mode necessary for resolution.

Keep the call simple. Identify yourself, confirm they received your email, and reiterate your intent to resolve the claim. Listen often. Talk little. Learn as much as possible to assess the risk in this case. You owe it to your client.

Specific Negotiation Techniques

Person to Person Contact – Experience shows person to person contact is needed to settle a case. This is typically done with phone calls.

Tone of voice – Tone of voice is critical to settlement – it must be a tone which conveys you want to settle the case if possible. At all times, be polite and courteous. If they call you "sir" or "Ma'am" reciprocate. Do not be overly formal, for a relaxed tone is conducive to getting them to relax and negotiate as opposed to posture.

Don't argue – As a general rule, don't argue the case. Arguing is "personal." It is not "listening," and it is not a discussion of substantive issues of liability or damages. There is a difference between substantive discussions of facts and arguing. When the other side argues, listen and acknowledge. Attorneys often want to argue their strong points on liability or damages. Arguing is them attempting to insert risk. Don't take the bait. Deflect arguments pointing out that liability is never certain and is always a risk for both sides. Deflect arguments on damages with substantive questions on damages. Damage evaluations on either side are always wrought with uncertainties leaving room for substantive questions.

Early Fair Offer of Settlement – Plaintiff's often put a high arbitrary value on their initial demand to insert risk to the defendant or because they believe the defendant will increase their reserves on a case. Likewise, defendants often put too low a value on a claim to entice a plaintiff to engage in negotiations.

Both sides are being arbitrary, unfair and reap what they sow. First offers from either side must be fair to initiate a meaningful reply. A fair offer typically begets a fair reply.

Never lie – Don't lie about anything. If you lose the trust you lose the ability to settle and you affect you reputation forever. Be truthful.

Time – Time is a critical. **<u>Always have enough time to talk and never feel pressured to compromise.</u>** If you are rushed in a conversation, you risk damaging the relationship. If you are rushed for time, you get hurried and make concessions or get angry which will hurt a negotiation. So, if you have limited time for a call, let the other side know what that time limit is, for example, begin by saying "Is this a good time for you?" or if they call you are limited, let them know "I only have fifteen minutes and if that's not enough, let's schedule a time now to get back in touch." Time is also a motivator for all sides to settle. Mediators often use the trial date and costs of trial to insert risk. The ERT negotiator can do the same.

Patience – A negotiator needs patience, patience to listen, patience to wait, patience not to respond negatively.

Take Responsibility

Mediation is rampant, yet there remains a need for common sense resolution by the attorneys involved, for rarely can a case be resolved if the attorney doesn't recommend it to their client. Ninety-five percent of all cases settle. As an attorney, do you part to get it settled earlier, not later.

About the Author

Chris Lisle received his law degree from the University of Arkansas in 1993 and began practicing law with his Father. He has over Twenty years' trial experience handling complex litigation including construction defects, personal injury, criminal, contracts, real estate.

After his father passed, he began doing early resolution for Walmart working as their lead negotiator on personal injury claims. He attended Harvard's basic negotiation course and their "Difficult Conversations" course.

He is a veteran of the US Army, having served in the 82nd Airborne Division. He completed Army Ranger School (awarded Ranger Tab, 1989); Army Parachute School, and German Parachute Wings. He's completed an Iron Distance Triathlon, Four Marathons, and climbed Mt. Kilimanjaro in Africa.

www.ingramcontent.com/pod-product-compliance
Lightning Source LLC
Chambersburg PA
CBHW071203220526
45468CB00003B/1149